CW00343178

GOOD OLD FASHIONED

SCHOOL DINNERS

This edition published in the United Kingdom in 2013 by
Portico Books
10 Southcombe Street
London
W14 0RA

An imprint of Anova Books Company Ltd

ISBN: 9781907554957

A CIP catalogue record for this book is available from
the British Library.

10 9 8 7 6 5 4 3 2 1

Printed and bound by Toppan Leefung Printing Ltd, China

This book can be ordered direct from the publisher at
www.anovabooks.com

**Dinner ladies
and school cooks
the country over,
I raise my scoop
in salute!**

PORTICO

BECKY THORN

RECIPES WORTH GOING BACK TO SCHOOL FOR!

GOOD OLD FASHIONED

SCHOOL DINNERS

THE GOOD, THE BAD AND THE SPOTTED DICK

CONTENTS

REGISTRATION

OK class, settle down, take your seats, get your textbooks out ... and let's begin eating some good old fashioned school dinners!

We're here to learn and what better way to start a new term than by cooking some delicious food that evokes that familiar, back-to-school feeling of queuing up in the dinner hall and watching the dinner lady ladle some gloopy treats onto your plate. The smell of whatever was on the menu that day filling the corridors and classrooms, making tummies rumble with hunger each time the lunch bell rang. Those were the days!

School dinners have always meant a great deal to me. As a teacher and a cook, they fuse together my two favourite subjects – education and food.

At home I have a very precious (if dog-eared!) notebook filled with handwritten recipes that once belonged to my mum. Folded neatly and tucked in between the pages of this book was a very tatty and stained piece of paper. It is a school newsletter from when I was at infant school and on the back of it the following lines are scribbled:

BUTTERSCOTCH TART
170g margarine
100ml milk
170g brown sugar
35g flour

Line a tin with pastry and bake. Melt margarine and milk, and boil – add sugar and flour – cook – allow to cool – spread on pastry.

Butterscotch tart was my favourite school dinner pudding and discovering this recipe set my mind into frantic motion: what other lovely school dinners could I find and share with my family? I knew somewhere I had a few simple recipes that a school cook friend of mine had written down for me. These became the foundation of my school dinners' recipe collection and it wasn't long before I had lots more of them jotted down and waiting patiently to be authentically re-created and served up.

In this book I hope you will find flavours that awaken fond memories of your days at school. For me, food is a fantastic way to time travel. A chance for your brain and stomach to reconnect with the tastes and smells of foods you used to eat all the time and, sadly, don't eat as often as you perhaps would like. Be honest, when was the last time you had jam roly-poly with lashings of hot, thick custard?

School dinners are such an important part of childhood – and are a huge aspect of our daily diet too. I remember children running around the playground excitedly telling one another that jam tarts were on the menu and to make sure they all get one before they disappear! It is a shame that we no longer treat ourselves to the smells and flavours we once enjoyed so much, now we've become proper grown ups.

So, pick a recipe you fancy, put on a pinny and try not to make too much of a mess. But don't worry if you do, that's half the fun. Tuck in ... and enjoy!

PIES

School pies were fantastic – sometimes crunchy, occasionally stodgy, but always delicious. Tasty toppings were cut through carefully and gave way to the slowly cooked fillings hiding underneath. Suet-topped steak and kidney pudding was a warming winter favourite, while the soft and seriously comforting cottage pie raised our spirits after a spelling test. Cobblers on the menu had us giggling and smirking as only teenagers can.

Each recipe feeds a family of four with seconds.

BEEF COBBLER

In cold winters, beef cobbler worked like a hot-water bottle, keeping many a school child warm. Cobblers (insert own schoolboy snigger here!) are delicious cheesy rounds, rather like scones, baked on top of a casserole. Their glossy exterior and cheesy crunch was pure heaven, and the perfect contrast to the soft, savoury meat underneath.

Add a little grated horseradish, dry mustard powder or dried herbs to the cobbler mixture for extra special flavour, especially if used as a topping for beef.

Ingredients

2 tbsp plain flour
Salt and pepper
500g stewing steak, cubed
2 tbsp vegetable oil
1 onion, finely chopped
300ml stock / water
3 carrots, chopped
175g self-raising flour
30g butter or marg
125g Cheddar cheese, grated
1 medium egg, beaten
1 tbsp milk
Beaten egg to glaze

1. Place the plain flour in a mixing bowl and season well. Toss the meat in the flour to coat well. Leave to one side for a few minutes.

2. Heat the oil in a large frying pan and add the floured beef. Cook until the beef is well browned and then add the onion. Continue to cook until the onion has softened. Add the stock or water then bring to barely simmering point. Reduce the heat, cover and leave for 2 hours, stirring occasionally.

3. Check the seasoning and add the carrots. Cover again and leave for a further 30 minutes. Meanwhile preheat the oven to 200°C/Gas 6.

4. Place the self-raising flour in a mixing bowl and rub in the

butter or margarine until the mixture resembles breadcrumbs. Stir in the cheese then use a round-ended palette knife to mix in the egg and enough milk to make the mixture come together. Use your hands to pat out the dough until about 2.5cm thick and cut out rounds using a large pastry cutter.

5. Place the cooked beef into a large oval baking dish and top with the cobbler rounds. Brush the topping with beaten egg and bake for 25 to 30 minutes until golden brown. Serve with mashed potatoes, green vegetables and extra delicious gravy!

TELL US A JOKE, MISS

Knock knock
Who's there?
Noah
Noah who?
Noah good place where I can get my car fixed?

50g butter

1 onion, finely
   chopped

3 carrots, chopped

450ml chicken stock

25g plain flour

Salt and pepper

Lemon juice

Fresh tarragon or
   parsley

500g cooked chicken,
   cubed

Shortcrust pastry
   (ready made OK!)

Milk or beaten egg
   to glaze

CHICKEN PIE

I loved chicken pie, but what a dilemma it used to cause me. Was I in a pastry-eating mood or a chicken-eating one? Which part did I eat first and which was saved for later?

Some days I would have done anything for an edge piece, which had more of the delicious crumbly pastry sitting on top of the juicy chicken, onion and carrot mixture. Flavoured with a dash of lemon juice and fresh herbs, the rich gravy from the pie used to moisten the mashed potatoes with which the pie was served.

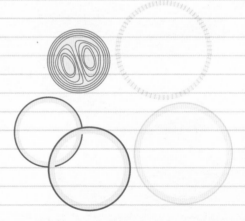

1. Preheat the oven to 200°C/Gas 6. Melt half the butter in a large frying pan and add the onion. Sweat the onion for 10 minutes until soft but not coloured. Add the carrots and toss in the butter and onion mixture. Pour in 150ml of stock and simmer gently until the stock has reduced to almost nothing. Place the onion and carrots in the bottom of a (yes, you've guessed it) rectangular pie or casserole dish.

2. Melt the remaining butter in a saucepan and stir in the flour. Keep stirring until the floury flavour has been cooked out. This will take a few minutes but no longer than 5. Gradually pour in the remaining stock, stirring constantly to prevent lumps (I know this is school dinners but some things are a little too authentic!). When all the stock is combined, simmer gently for another 5 minutes.

3. Season your sauce with a good pinch of salt and freshly ground black pepper. A squeeze of lemon juice and a handful of chopped tarragon or parsley wouldn't go amiss either. Arrange the chicken in the pie dish and pour over the sauce. Give it a stir to combine the flavours.

4. Top the pie with shortcrust pastry. Brush with milk or beaten egg and bake for 25 to 30 minutes or until the pie crust is golden brown.

PLEASE SIR, CAN I HAVE SOME MORE?

If you want to make this pie extra special, you could add white wine instead of stock when making the sauce. Add what you want! If you have mushrooms, add them. It will give the children something to pick out too!

2 tbsp vegetable oil

1 onion, finely
    chopped

3 carrots, chopped

3 sticks of celery,
    chopped

500g lean minced
    beef

2 tsp Marmite

300ml beef stock

Salt and pepper

1 tbsp fresh herbs or
    1 tsp dried herbs

Shortcrust pastry
    (ready made OK!)

Milk or beaten egg
    to glaze

MINCED-MEAT PIE

Slow-cooked with carrots, onions and celery until rich and delicious and meltingly tender, the minced beef in this pie is then topped with a golden pastry crust. There were the usual playground rumours that it was minced squirrel or kangaroo in the pie but I didn't care; covered in plenty of gravy it always tasted great.

Despite the vegetables in the pie it was very popular. School cooks were savvy and knew to cut them up finely and cook them until they had all but disappeared, leaving nothing for the fussier children to pick out.

1. Preheat the oven to 200°C/Gas 6. Heat half the oil in a large pan and add the onion, carrots and celery. Stir to coat and cook gently until softened but not coloured. Remove to a mixing bowl and cover.

2. Heat the remaining oil in the pan, add the minced beef and cook until browned. Keep the mince moving and break up any large lumps with your wooden spoon. School cooks sometimes missed this bit out and these lumps may in part have led to the squirrel pie rumours.

3. Return the vegetables to the pan and stir well. Stir the Marmite into the stock and add to the pan. Keep stirring to loosen the stickiness on the bottom of the pan. If you are using dried herbs, add them now. Bring to a simmer then reduce the heat until the surface of the mixture barely moves. Cover and leave for at least an hour and a half, stirring occasionally, until the stock has reduced to a thick gravy and the meat is very tender. If necessary, increase the heat and reduce the sauce further, stirring. Check for seasoning and add fresh herbs now, if using.

4. Arrange the meat in a large rectangular baking dish. Top with shortcrust pastry and brush with milk or beaten egg. Bake for 25 to 30 minutes or until golden brown. Serve with boiled potatoes, peas or beans and lashings of gravy.

PLEASE SIR, CAN I HAVE SOME MORE?

To make this pie a little more interesting you could add a glug of red wine instead of using boring old stock.

- INGREDIENTS -

2 tbsp vegetable oil

1 onion, finely
chopped

500g lean minced
beef

400g can chopped
tomatoes

150g frozen peas

300ml beef stock

Salt and pepper

1kg mashing
potatoes, peeled
and cubed

Butter

Milk

COTTAGE PIE

A layer of soft creamy mash topped the rich and tender minced beef in this well-known pie. This was comfort food at its best, and especially popular with children who had recently lost a tooth, through natural means or otherwise.

The uninitiated might expect this to be the same as the minced-meat pie with a mashed potato topping but no, cottage pie is quite different, with peas and tomatoes in the filling.

1. Preheat the oven to 200°C/Gas 6. Heat half the oil in a large pan and add the onion. Stir to coat and cook gently until softened but not coloured. Remove to a mixing bowl and cover.

2. Heat the remaining oil in the pan, add the beef and cook until browned. Keep the mince moving and break up any large lumps with your wooden spoon. Return the onion to the pan and stir well. Add the tomatoes and peas, slosh in the stock and stir to loosen the stickiness on the bottom of the pan. Bring to a simmer then reduce the heat until the surface of the meat just shivers. Cover and leave for at least an hour and a half, stirring occasionally, until the stock has reduced to a thick gravy and the meat is very tender. If necessary, increase the heat and reduce the sauce further, stirring. Season to taste.

3. With about 20 minutes to go, put the potatoes on to boil. When cooked through, drain well and leave in the colander over the warm pan to dry out a little. If you have a potato ricer please use as it virtually guarantees lump-free mash. If you don't have one, put it on your birthday list and get a child or a guest to mash the potato for you. Doing this gives you time to have a quick mouthful of wine and prevents them from complaining that the mash is lumpy as they made it! Stir in butter and milk to taste.

4. Arrange the meat in a large baking dish and top with the potatoes. Bake for 25 minutes or until the topping is golden and bubbly.

TOP 10

Excuses For NOT Doing Homework

1. The dog ate it.
2. I couldn't find the answers anywhere.
3. The house was cold so we had to set fire to it to keep warm.
4. Homework? I thought you were joking!
5. I was abducted by aliens and they only brought me back this morning.
6. It was in my backpack this morning, someone must have stolen it.
7. It fell out of my bag as I helped an old lady across the road.
8. My dad accidentally put it in his briefcase.
9. I had better things to do.
10. I didn't want to make the rest of the class look bad by doing so well.

500g coley or
  haddock
600ml milk
1 bay leaf
Peppercorns
250g bag spinach
Nutmeg
1kg mashing
  potatoes,
  peeled / cubed
1 tbsp butter
2 tbsp plain flour
Salt and white
  pepper
Butter
Milk

FISH PIE

Although an island nation, we had fish just once a week on a Friday, so this rich and tasty recipe was always popular. Soft chunks of white fish coated in a savoury white sauce, flavoured with bay leaves and black pepper, were topped with smooth mash. Sometimes the cook added a layer of spinach seasoned with nutmeg, which made the pie look more appealing and gave the fussy children something to pick out.

1. Preheat the oven to 200°C/Gas 6. Place the fish in a shallow saucepan and cover with the milk. Add a bay leaf and a few peppercorns. Bring slowly to the boil then remove from the heat and rest for 5 minutes or so. Lift the fish onto a plate and strain and reserve the cooking liquor. Discard the peppercorns and bay leaf.

2. Rinse the spinach and place in a hot pan with no additional water. Cook, stirring, until wilted then place in a sieve to drain. Lay the spinach in the bottom of a rectangular casserole or pie dish. Grate a little nutmeg over the spinach if you wish.

3. Put the potatoes on to boil, then make the sauce. Melt the butter in a saucepan and stir in the flour. Cook this mixture for a few minutes, reduce the heat and gradually add the reserved cooking liquor, stirring all the time, until the sauce has a creamy consistency. Season to taste. Flake the fish into the sauce, removing stray bones, then plonk in the spinach.

4. Mash your potatoes with a little butter and milk and, using a spatula, smooth over the fish mixture. Rough up the surface of the fish pie with a fork. No ice-cream scoops here: it was one way of telling if it was fish or cottage pie – if the smell didn't give it away, that is! Bake for 25 minutes or until the mash potato is golden.

PLEASE SIR, CAN I HAVE SOME MORE?

If you want to make this pie really special you could use some salmon fillets or add a few prawns to make a more varied filling. I'm not a fan of the fish-cheese combination but if you are, then making a cheesy mash topping might just float your boat!

Shortcrust pastry
  (ready made OK!)
1 medium egg
150ml milk
Pepper
½ tsp mustard
  powder
150g strong
  Cheddar cheese,
  grated
Extra Cheddar
  for the topping

CHEESE FLAN

With its soft and creamy filling, cheesy top layer and crumbly pastry case, cheese flan was good, simple fare. This is a quick and easy recipe which was always served on a Friday, when meat was off the menu.

Please remember cheese flan must be served with boiled potatoes and canned tomatoes. Oh, and never, ever, refer to this as a quiche!

1. Preheat the oven to 200°C/Gas 6. Line a small flan ring with pastry and blind bake for 10 minutes. (Baking blind means lining the pastry case with baking parchment or greaseproof paper and filling the case with baking beans.) Bake, cool slightly and remove the paper and beans. Turn the oven down to 180°C/Gas 4.

2. Mix together the egg, milk, pepper and mustard powder. Stir in the grated cheese. Pour this into the cooled pie case and make sure the cheese is evenly distributed.

3. Grate a little more cheese over the flan and bake for 20 minutes until the cheese flan is golden brown on top and has a slight wobble to the filling. While cooking the flan, put your new potatoes on to boil and open a can of tomatoes and warm through.

SCIENCE

1. Diamonds are a form of which chemical element?
2. The longest bone in the human body is?
3. Relating to flat-screen televisions and monitors, what does LCD stand for?
4. What is the mathematical series that starts 0,1,1,2,3,5,8,13,21 called?
5. Which subatomic particles are found in the nucleus of an atom?
6. Which sugar is found in milk?
7. What is the largest species of big cat in South America?
8. What did Wilhelm Conrad Röntgen discover by accident on 8 November 1895?
9. In trigonometry, what is calculated by the adjacent over the hypotenuse?
10. What is the colour of copper sulphate?

Check the answers on pages 94–5

2 tbsp plain flour

Salt and pepper

500g stewing
   steak, cubed

125g lamb kidneys,
   trimmed, cored
   and cubed

2 tbsp vegetable oil

1 onion, finely
   chopped

300ml beef stock

Suet pastry
   (ready made OK!)

STEAK AND KIDNEY PUDDING

With its soft, puffy suet crust, covering tender chunks of meat in rich, dark gravy, steak and kidney pudding was heavenly and one of the all-time best. Although it seemed the role of a school cook was to fill us up, it always surprised me that pies only came with tops and never bottoms, and this was true of steak and kidney pudding. The crust was like one enormous dumpling laid on top of the meat mixture and the long, slow cooking process ensured both the crust and the meat were wonderfully soft and done to perfection.

1. Place the flour in a mixing bowl and season well. Toss the steak and kidneys in the flour to coat well. Leave to one side for a few minutes.

2. Heat the oil in a large frying pan, add the floured beef and the kidneys and cook until browned. (You may need to do this in two batches to prevent the pan from becoming overcrowded.) Transfer to a large, lidded casserole dish.

3. Add the onion to the frying pan and cook gently until softened, then transfer to the casserole dish. Add the stock to the frying pan and scrape any sticky bits from the bottom of the pan. Pour the stock into the casserole dish, place on the hob and bring to a simmer. Reduce the heat, cover and leave for half an hour, stirring occasionally. Meanwhile preheat the oven to 180°C/Gas 4.

4. Cover the steak and kidneys with the suet pastry, pressing down to make sure it is in contact with the meat, and then replace the casserole lid. Bake for an hour and a half in the oven. Do not be tempted to peek or remove the casserole lid as the steam created in the pot will cause the suet crust to rise. If your casserole lid doesn't fit tightly, seal the edges with a flour and water paste. Serve with carrots, peas and thick, thick gravy.

PLEASE SIR, CAN I HAVE SOME MORE?

You could make this much more interesting by adding chunks of Portobello mushrooms, a little red wine, stout or even oysters.

1 tbsp vegetable oil

1 onion, diced

2 large flat mushrooms, sliced and diced

Plain flour for rolling out

Shortcrust pastry

500g sausages, skins removed

½ tsp mustard powder

1 tsp tomato purée

½ red pepper, deseeded / finely chopped

Salt and pepper

1 egg, beaten

SAUSAGE PLAIT

Although in essence a giant sausage roll, the sausage plait was not quite so straightforward as it first appeared, harbouring as it did a couple of unusual ingredients beneath its crisp and golden pastry shell.

Mushrooms were considered a little racy in my school days, but if the mushrooms were bordering on exotic what they added next was almost unheard of. I am sure this was the first time I ever came across peppers or, as our school cook very correctly called them when we pointed and asked 'What's that?', capsicums. With its flavoursome savoury filling, this is delicious hot or cold.

1. Preheat the oven to 200°C/Gas 6. In a large frying pan, heat the oil and add the diced onion. Cook until the onion is softened and has begun to turn golden. Add the mushrooms and cook for a further 5 minutes. Leave to cool for a few moments.

2. Roll out a 24 x 20cm rectangle of pastry. Transfer to a baking sheet. Place the sausage meat in a large bowl and add the mustard powder and tomato purée. Add the diced red peppers, cooled onion and mushrooms and season to taste. Using your hands, mix together well and place lengthways in the middle of the pastry rectangle.

3. Cut strips 2.5cm wide in a feather pattern down either side of the pastry. Fold alternating strips across the sausage mixture from top to bottom. Tuck in and tidy the first and last strips, trimming where needed. Brush with the beaten egg and bake for 30 to 35 minutes. If the pastry is browning too quickly, cover with a piece of foil. Serve with canned tomatoes and mash.

PLEASE SIR, CAN I HAVE SOME MORE?

This is lovely eaten cold on a sunny evening. If you do this, please feel free to ignore the previous serving suggestion of canned toms and mash and go for watercress salad and glass of crisp white wine!

PIES

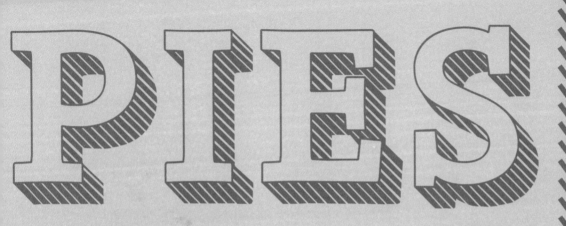

Pastry would always make an appearance at school dinners. If it was a tart for pudding then it was not a pie for main, but this doesn't mean the meals were not filling. Pasta and rice made us feel cosmopolitan, served with cowboy casserole, Bolognese or chicken curry. Meatballs were sung about, toad in the hole was worried over and spam fritters were raised to iconic status.

Each recipe feeds a family of four with seconds.

CHICKEN SUPREME

For our school cook, chicken supreme with rice, peas and carrots was the height of cosmopolitan sophistication. Although it could be criticized for being rather too beige, the flavour of this dish more than made up for it and we were happy to tuck in to the succulent chunks of tender chicken and mushrooms.

Ideally, we would have used just a fork to eat it in the same way as the stars did on American TV programmes such as 'Little House on the Prairie' but we all knew this was a step too far. Much as we would have liked to see a dinner lady explode, it might have delayed our pudding.

2 tbsp olive oil
Knob of butter
2 tbsp plain flour
Salt and pepper
½ tsp paprika
4 chicken breasts or
  6 thighs, cubed
1 onion, finely diced
6 mushrooms, sliced
300ml chicken stock
A squeeze of lemon
  juice
Fresh parsley
  to serve

1. Heat 1 tbsp of oil and the butter in a large frying pan. Place the flour in a mixing bowl and season well with salt, pepper and the paprika. Toss the chicken cubes in the flour, shake off any excess and gently lay in the hot pan. Cook the chicken until golden and crispy on the outside (do not worry if not completely cooked through.) Remove to a separate plate and keep warm.

2. Add the remaining oil to the pan with the onion. (Don't panic if there are still flour bits in the pan, it will help the flavour of the finished dish.) Cook the onion until soft and beginning to brown around the edges. Add the mushrooms and continue cooking until they give out their juices. When this happens add any remaining seasoned flour and cook for a minute or so, stirring all the time.

3. Pour in the stock and the mixture will thicken slightly. If it thickens too much, add a little water or milk at this point. Return the chicken pieces to the pan and stir well. Continue cooking for another 5 minutes or until the chicken is cooked through. Taste the sauce and season again. A squeeze of lemon will lift the flavour.

4. If beige bothers you please feel free to add baby spinach or peeled and chopped fresh tomatoes at the final moment. Be careful not to cook these to a mush though or the result will be an even nastier colour! Sprinkle with parsley and serve with rice and vegetables. Put on reruns of 'Little House on the Prairie' and eat with just a fork.

- INGREDIENTS -

450g good-quality
  chipolatas
1 tbsp oil
125g plain flour
2 medium eggs
300ml milk
Salt and pepper

TOAD IN THE HOLE

No toads and no holes, just lots of lovely sausages encased in crispy batter. It's a simple recipe but the result is delicious and satisfying, especially when served with lashings and lashings of gravy. This was a meal where lots of swaps went on: you can have my sausage if you give me your batter. I could never decide which I liked more!

1. Preheat the oven to 240°C/Gas 9 and turn on the grill to heat through. Grill the sausages until cooked through. Place a large deep baking tin with the oil in the oven and wait until the pan is smoking hot.

2. Sieve the flour into a large bowl, break in the eggs, add the milk and whisk until combined. Season the batter well.

3. Light a ring on the hob. Take the tin from the oven and place over the heat to keep hot. Working very quickly, pour the batter into the hot tin and arrange the sausages as evenly as you can. Return the tin to the oven and bake for 20 minutes until risen and golden. Do not peek or you will let the heat out of the oven.

4. Serve with gravy and green beans. You can put these on to boil the day before if you want a retro green bean experience but I suggest a more modern 3 to 5 minutes.

Playground Rhymes

How many do you remember?

1. 'Ring a Ring O'Roses'
2. 'London Bridge'
3. 'One Potato'
4. 'Oranges and Lemons'
5. 'Pat-a-cake, Pat-a-cake'
6. 'Follow the Leader'
7. 'Row, Row, Row Your Boat'
8. 'Mary, Mary, Quite Contrary'
9. 'Jack and Jill'
10. 'She'll Be Coming 'Round the Mountain When She Comes'

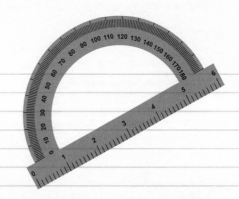

PLEASE SIR, CAN I HAVE SOME MORE?

The key to getting the batter to rise and crisp up is in the temperature. Heat the tin until smoking hot before adding the batter. Keep it hot on the hob while you fill it, then place back in the oven ASAP to puff up!

2 tbsp plain flour
Salt and pepper
Pinch of mixed herbs
500g stewing steak,
   cubed
2 tbsp vegetable oil
1 onion, finely
   chopped
400g can chopped
   tomatoes
½ tsp granulated
   sugar
Beef stock or water
2 carrots, chopped
Celery, parsnips or
   swede, chopped

BEEF CASSEROLE

Eating beef casserole felt like being hugged from the inside. Warming and comforting, it was delicious to eat with mashed potatoes and, just now and then, extra ladles of gravy. The vegetables in the casserole changed with the seasons, adding variety and interest to our lunches.

1. Place the flour into a large bowl and season well. A school cook may have added dried mixed herbs too if she felt she could get away with it. Toss the meat in the flour to coat well. Leave to one side for a few minutes.

2. Heat the oil in a large pan. Add the floured beef and cook until well browned. Add the onion and fry until softened. Add the chopped tomatoes and sugar as this will bring out the tomatoey taste.

3. Add enough stock or water to just cover the beef and bring to barely simmering point. (Sometimes a squeeze of mustard or a slug of Worcestershire sauce would make its way in too.) Reduce the heat right down, cover and leave for at least 2 hours, stirring occasionally.

4. Check the seasoning and add the carrots and any other vegetables. Cover again and leave for a further 30 minutes. Serve from a large aluminium bowl using a ladle. Mash and gravy are a must too!

PLEASE SIR, CAN I HAVE SOME MORE?

This is the perfect recipe for a cold winter's day. Prepare the casserole after breakfast and leave it to cook while you go out for a bracing walk. On your return you will be greeted by a wonderful aroma and the prospect of a warming and delicious lunch, as we once were.

GEOGRAPHY

1. Which island group includes Ibiza, Menorca and Majorca?
2. Machu Picchu is in which country?
3. Dulles Airport serves which US city?
4. The Victoria Falls are on which river?
5. Which landlocked sea is 422m (1,385ft) below sea level?
6. What is created when the loop of a meander of a river is cut off and the river diverted on a different course?
7. Of which republic are English, Malay, Mandarin Chinese and Tamil the four official languages?
8. Which country's flag has a cedar tree?
9. Mauritius is found in which ocean?
10. Who developed the most-used projection for maps of the world in 1569?

Check the answers on pages 94–5

CHICKEN CASSEROLE

2 tbsp plain flour

Salt and pepper

1 chicken, cut into 8 portions

2 tbsp vegetable oil

4 rashers streaky bacon, chopped

1 onion, finely chopped

1 garlic clove, crushed

4 large mushrooms, cut into quarters

Stock or water

1 carrot, chopped

A squeeze of lemon juice

We knew it was a special day if chicken casserole was on the menu. Chicken was a meat saved for occasions: not for us the deep-fried, reconstituted and bright-orange-hued breaded shapes, but real chicken. We knew that because ours came with the bones still attached.

This casserole is flavoured with bacon, onion, garlic and carrot to make a really tasty gravy round the chicken. Add a little lemon juice to enhance the flavour and use stock instead of water to achieve the richest gravy.

1. Place the flour in a large bowl and season well. Toss the chicken in the flour to completely coat. Leave to one side for a few minutes.

2. Heat the oil in a large pan, add the floured chicken and fry until the chicken pieces have taken on a golden colour. Remove the chicken to a plate and rest. In the chickeny oil, fry the bacon until crispy and then add the onion and garlic. Continue to cook until the onion is golden and melting.

3. Add the mushrooms and fry until soft. Tip in any remaining seasoned flour and cook for 1 minute. Return the chicken to the pan with the bacon, onions and mushrooms. Add the stock or water to cover and bring to barely simmering point. Add the carrot and reduce the heat. Cover and leave for an hour, stirring occasionally.

4. Check the chicken is cooked through and adjust the seasoning if necessary. A squeeze of lemon will zing up this dish no end. Serve with roast potatoes and bright-green cabbage, briefly cooked and still crunchy. Cabbage does not need a fortnight in a nuclear reactor to make it edible! Eat as neatly as you can but feel free to suck the bones to get the last remaining bits of meat off!

2 tbsp plain flour

Salt and pepper

750g leg of lamb,
cubed

2 onions, thinly
sliced

4 large potatoes,
thinly sliced

Handful of thyme
leaves

500ml beef stock or
water

Butter

LANCASHIRE HOTPOT

Crusty and brown on the outside and meltingly tender on the inside, Lancashire hotpot was that rare creature: a regional dish on the school menu. I had no idea where Lancashire was but I was eternally grateful to it. This is a simple dish of lamb, onions and potatoes, layered and baked until soft, but what a wonderful combination. Deciding if the potato should be devoured before the meat or after was a dilemma I faced with lip-licking enthusiasm. This is one of those dishes you always went back for seconds for. And sometimes thirds, if there was ever any left!

1. Preheat the oven to 180°C/Gas 4. Place the flour in a large bowl and season well. Toss the meat in the flour to completely coat. Leave to one side for a few minutes. (The flour is important as it makes your gravy.) Mix the onions with the floured lamb cubes.

2. Place one-third of the potato slices in the bottom of a lidded casserole dish or hotpot if you have one. Arrange half the lamb and onions on top. Sprinkle with a little thyme, then add another layer of potatoes and the remaining meat.

3. Finish with a layer of potatoes, taking time to overlap them neatly as school cook pride is at stake. Try to make it look reasonably tidy.

4. Add stock or water until it comes just under the top layer of potatoes. Dot the top with a knob of butter, cover and bake for at least 2 hours. Preheat the grill 10 minutes before taking the hotpot out.

5. Remove the lid and dot again with a little more butter. Pop under a hot grill until the top is brown and crispy. Serve in front of a large map of the UK so everyone knows from whence this wondrous dish originates.

TELL US A JOKE, MISS

What's yellow and swings through the jungle smelling of almonds?

Tarzipan

- INGREDIENTS -

375g macaroni
25g butter
25g plain flour
300ml milk
125g Cheddar
  cheese, grated
Salt and pepper
1 fresh tomato, sliced

MACARONI CHEESE

Still heartily enjoyed by children all over the country today, macaroni cheese will probably always be a school dinner classic. The soft tubes of pasta were coated in oozing, creamy cheese sauce and sprinkled with extra grated cheese for a delicious melted topping. Each portion was adorned with a slice of fresh tomato and however hard you tried to remove the tomato, the melted cheese welded the garnish to the top. This was, and still is, a very canny way to get fresh vegetables inside the tummies of unwilling children!

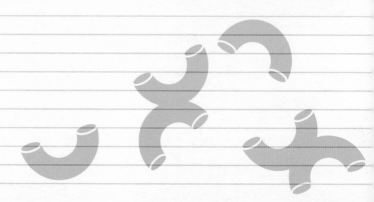

1. Preheat the oven to 180°C/Gas 4. Cook the macaroni in salted boiling water until just cooked through. Drain and leave to one side.

2. To make the cheese sauce, melt the butter in a large pan, add the flour and cook for a minute. Add the milk and whisk vigorously to prevent lumps. Cook until the sauce visibly thickens. Once thick, stir in most of the grated cheese. Season to taste.

3. Stir in the macaroni and make sure it is well combined. Tip the mixture into a large rectangular baking dish. Scatter over the remaining cheese and garnish each portion with a slice of tomato. Bake in the oven for 20 minutes. Serve with a salad of grated carrot and raisins (I kid you not!).

Best TV programmes set at school

These are my favourite school TV shows
I used to watch after school. Did you?

1. *Grange Hill*
2. *Beverly Hills, 90210*
3. *Saved by the Bell*
4. *Degrassi High*
5. *Glee*
6. *The Inbetweeners*
7. *Heartbreak High*
8. *Buffy the Vampire Slayer*
9. *Summer Heights High*
10. *Teachers*

CAULIFLOWER CHEESE

1 large cauliflower,
  cut into florets

25g butter

25g plain flour

1 tsp dried mustard
  powder

300ml milk

125g strong Cheddar
  cheese, grated

Salt and pepper

4 tbsp fresh
  breadcrumbs

Serving it in a sea of lovely cheesy sauce was a great way to encourage children to enjoy cauliflower. The crunchy toasted cheese and breadcrumb topping was the best bit, and provided the perfect contrast to the tender cauliflower and smooth sauce beneath. I always saved the topping for the final, delectable mouthful. Serve with whatever else takes your fancy!

1. Place the cauliflower florets in salted boiling water until just cooked. Drain and leave to one side.

2. To make the cheese sauce, melt the butter in a large pan, add the flour and mustard powder; cook for 1 minute. Add the milk and whisk vigorously to prevent lumps. Cook until the sauce visibly thickens. Once thick, stir in most of the grated cheese. Season to taste.

3. Stir in the cooked cauliflower and make sure it is well combined. Tip the mixture into a large rectangular baking dish. Scatter over the remaining cheese and the breadcrumbs. Flash under a hot grill until the cheese bubbles and the breadcrumbs are toasted. Serve as a side dish with pork chops or eat as a main meal with a big green salad.

ENTERTAINMENT

1. The character Betty Draper is from which acclaimed television series?
2. Henry Hill is the wise guy in which film?
3. 'You Give Love a Bad Name' and 'Livin' on a Prayer' were early hits for which band?
4. What are Romeo and Juliet's surnames?
5. 'Who loves ya, baby?' was a catchphrase of which 1970s lollipop-sucking detective?
6. Who played Maximus Decimus Meridius in a 2000 Ridley Scott film?
7. What was Elvis Presley's middle name?
8. Despite the legend, in which film is 'Play it again, Sam' never actually said?
9. First performed in 1918, who composed 'The Planets Suite'?
10. In 2009, which band released the album 'West Ryder Pauper Lunatic Asylum'?

Check the answers on pages 94–5

DID YOU KNOW?

Anomia: The term for those moments when you have a word on the tip of your tongue and you can't quite remember it!

340g can Spam
100g plain flour
Ice-cold sparkling
   mineral water
Pinch of salt
Vegetable oil for
   frying
Plain flour for
   dusting

SPAM FRITTERS

The guiltiest guilty pleasure of them all! Spam fritters are something many profess not to like but secretly enjoy. I, however, would gladly shout from the rooftops that I adore Spam fritters! With their crispy coating and blisteringly hot Spam beneath, fritters are the stuff dreams are made of!

1. Place the Spam can into the fridge to chill for several hours before starting this recipe. Remove the Spam from the can and slice into 1cm thick portions. Return to the fridge until needed.

2. In a large bowl, mix together the flour and sparkling mineral water until the batter is the thickness of double cream. (If you don't have sparkling mineral water, add 1 tsp of bicarbonate of soda to the flour instead and use plain water.) The secret to this batter is to use ice-cold water. Add a pinch of salt. Put the oil on to heat. You can shallow- or deep-fry – depending on bravery or your equipment.

3. Take the Spam out of the fridge and coat very lightly in flour. Remove any excess by patting the Spam gently (the flour will help the batter to stick). Dip the Spam into the batter and lay gently in the oil. The oil needs to be fairly hot or your batter will become soggy.

4. The fritters will take about 2 minutes to cook on each side and about 3 or 4 minutes if you are deep-frying. Remove from the oil when golden brown. Drain well. Serve with mash and beans or peas. Ketchup is an optional accompaniment.

TELL US A JOKE, MISS

Knock knock
Who's there?
Albert
Albert who?
**Albert you don't know
who this is**

Silliest Collective Nouns

1. **Apes** A shrewdness of apes
2. **Magpies** A tittering of magpies
3. **Owls** A parliament of owls
4. **Moles** A mumble of moles
5. **Ravens** An unkindness of ravens
6. **Rook** A building of rooks
7. **Bears** A sloth of bears
8. **Caterpillars** An army of caterpillars
9. **Woodpeckers** A descent of woodpeckers
10. **Racoons** A nursery of racoons

1 onion, chopped
Vegetable oil for
  frying
Several carrots, diced
500g lean minced
  beef
400g can chopped
  tomatoes
Generous pinch of
  dried mixed herbs
Worcestershire sauce
Salt and pepper
Beef stock
300g dried spaghetti

SPAGHETTI BOLOGNESE

When we had spag bol at school I always felt like it was the fanciest dish on the planet! I remember the rich ragú sauce was always stirred into the short lengths of spaghetti, but you can serve yours on top if you prefer!

1. Brown the onion in a little oil in a saucepan and then add the carrots. Tip in the minced beef and cook until the mince is no longer in lumps. Stir in the canned tomatoes, herbs, Worcestershire sauce and seasoning. Cover with stock (school cooks may have just used water or cabbage water!).

2. Bring to the simmer and reduce the heat until the surface of the mince mixture just quivers. Leave to cook for at least 2 hours, stirring occasionally. Add more water only if needed. I think the key to this mince recipe was long-slow cooking. It is the way the Italians have been making the world's most beloved ragù for years.

3. Twenty minutes before you want to eat, place the dried spaghetti in a large pan of boiling water (with a pinch of salt) and keep checking until cooked. Just before serving, stir the spaghetti into the sauce. That's it! Buon appetito!

TELL US A JOKE, MISS

Where did the spaghetti go to dance?
The meat ball!

(Apologies for this one!)

PLEASE SIR, CAN I HAVE SOME MORE?

Occasionally if the pasta was too exhausting there was a British version of this dish. Trim the crust off a slice of bread and cut into four triangles. Heat lard or bacon fat in a pan until very hot and then fry the bread on both sides. (Hot fat will soak in less than cool fat). Place the cooked mince in an oblong metal tray. Arrange the fried bread attractively over the mince (one per portion). Ring the bell and off you go!

500g lean mince
(lamb or beef)

100g fresh
breadcrumbs

100g finely grated
Cheddar cheese

A pinch of dried
mixed herbs

1 medium egg,
beaten

Salt and pepper

1 tbsp vegetable oil

300ml sieved
tomatoes (passata)

300ml beef stock

MEATBALLS

A dish so revered they wrote a song about it: 'On top of spaghetti, all covered in cheese, I once lost my meatball when somebody sneezed'.

These tasty little balls of herby meat were simmered in a rich tomato sauce and served with spaghetti, or potatoes and vegetables. So popular were meatballs that the dinner ladies had to count them on to the plates to ensure everyone had a fair portion. Befriending or engaging the dinner lady in conversation could, if you were lucky, result in a miscount and an extra meatball or two. But be careful not to push your luck!

1. In a large bowl, combine the mince, breadcrumbs, cheese, herbs, egg and seasoning until well mixed. Using damp hands, pinch off walnut-sized pieces of mixture and roll to create ball shapes. Place to one side until all the meatballs are made.

2. Heat the oil in a large frying pan and add the meatballs. Do not move in the pan for 5 minutes otherwise your meatballs will disintegrate. This will seal them. Turn gently every few minutes until completely browned.

3. Add the passata and enough stock to come just half way up the meatballs. Simmer gently for 20 minutes until the meatballs are cooked through. Serve with spaghetti and grated cheese so you can sing the song, or boiled potatoes and greens if you don't want the musical accompaniment.

Girls' Names of the 1950s and Now

1950	2013
1. Margaret	Olivia
2. Linda	Ruby
3. Mary	Chloe
4. Susan	Emily
5. Deborah	Sophie
6. Barbara	Jessica
7. Joan	Grace
8. Christine	Lily
9. Patricia	Amelia
10. Carol	Evie

500g lambs' or
   calves' liver
2 tbsp plain flour
Salt and pepper
1 tsp dried mixed or
   2 tsp fresh herbs
Knob of butter
1 tbsp vegetable oil
1 onion, finely
   chopped
350ml vegetable or
   chicken stock
250g streaky bacon

LIVER AND BACON

Seeing rolls of crispy bacon lined up on a silver tray made my heart leap, knowing that liver was on the menu. The thick, tasty gravy coating the fluffy mash had a depth of flavour unparalleled in other school meals. The glutton in me also knew that seconds of liver were always going to be forthcoming as others weren't so enthusiastic about it, and if I was lucky there would be seconds of bacon too. Handled badly, liver can quickly resemble shoe leather, both in texture and shape, but we were very fortunate to have a cook who knew that care must be taken.

1. Preheat the oven to 150°C/Gas 2. In the past liver was soaked in milk to temper the stronger flavours, especially from pigs' or ox liver. If you want to do this, that's fine (especially if cooking for liver virgins) but it shouldn't be necessary for school dinner veterans.

2. Trim the liver, removing any tubes or membrane. I don't want to put you off but they can be very chewy! Slice into thin escalopes if you want this school cook style or just cut into 1cm thick slices.

3. Combine the flour, seasoning and dried herbs on a plate. Coat the liver slices in the flour, patting off the excess. Heat the butter and oil in a frying pan. Fry the liver briefly to give it a golden crust, then place in a large casserole dish.

4. Fry the onion in the same pan, adding a little more oil if you need it. Once the onion has softened and browned, add any remaining flour and cook for a further minute. Add the stock and stir until the mixture thickens slightly. Pour over the liver and top with a little more stock to barely cover, if needed. Cover and cook for around 90 minutes.

5. While the casserole is cooking make the streaky bacon rolls. Using the back of a knife, stretch the rashers until twice their original length. Cut each rasher in half and roll up into a cylinder. Place on a baking tray. With half an hour to go place these rolls in the oven to bake alongside the liver and onions. Serve with a big scoop or two of creamy mash smothered with thick tasty gravy and a streaky bacon roll on the side. Seconds, anyone?

2 tbsp plain flour
Salt and pepper
4 chicken breasts,
   cubed
2 tbsp vegetable oil
1 onion, finely
   chopped
1 garlic clove,
   crushed
1–1½ tbsp curry
   powder (your
   choice of strength)
1 apple, peeled and
   chopped
A handful of raisins
300ml chicken stock
Lemon juice

CHICKEN CURRY

There is nothing authentic about this dish but it still tastes wonderful
– fruity and spicy all at the same time! As a school dinner, part of the
attraction that made this dish something to look forward to was the fact
that it was served with rice – a nice change from potatoes!

1. Place the flour in a large bowl and season well with the salt and pepper. Toss the chicken in the flour and coat well. Leave to one side for a few minutes. Make a cup of tea.

2. Heat the oil in a large pan, add the floured chicken and cook until the chicken pieces have taken on a golden colour. Remove the chicken to a plate and rest. Add the onion and garlic to the chickeny oil. Continue to cook until the onion is golden and melting. Breath in that smell!

3. Add the curry powder and cook until the spices are no longer raw. Return the chicken to the pan with the apple and raisins. Add enough stock to cover the meat and bring to barely simmering point. Turn the heat right down, cover and leave for half an hour, stirring occasionally.

4. Check the chicken is cooked and adjust the seasoning, if necessary. Add a squeeze of lemon juice. Serve with rice and ladle the curry into the middle from enough height so you might get froth on it. Yum!

QUIZ TIME

ART & LITERATURE

1. Which American abstract artist is best known for his 'drip paintings'?
2. The Bennet family appear in which Jane Austen novel?
3. Who created the famous sculptures 'The Thinker' and 'The Kiss'?
4. Who was the father of Goneril and Cordelia?
5. How are the sisters Meg, Jo, Beth and Amy described in the title of an 1868 novel?
6. Who painted 'The Laughing Cavalier'?
7. Which literary characters set out on a journey from the Tabard Inn in London?
8. Who is the Greek Goddess of Love?
9. The Meissen factory in Germany was manufacturer of which type of ceramic?
10. Who wrote the 'Twilight' series of novels?

Check the answers on pages 94–5

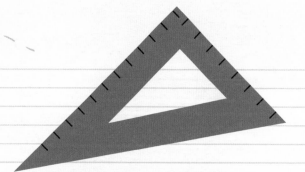

TELL US A JOKE, MISS

Why did the rubber chicken cross the road?

She wanted to stretch her legs!

450g good-quality
chipolatas
2 large baking
potatoes
3 tbsp vegetable oil
Salt and pepper
1 large onion, finely
chopped
Plain flour
300ml beef stock
or water
400g can chopped
tomatoes
400g can baked
beans
Worcestershire
sauce

COWBOY CASSEROLE

Cowboy casserole, a wonderful fusion of sausages and beans in a rich and savoury tomato sauce, topped with chunks of golden potato. Doesn't that sound marvellous? Right, enough of this waffle, let's just get started!

1. Preheat the oven to 200°C/Gas 6 and heat the grill. Grill the sausages until cooked through. Cut each one into three or four pieces and place in a large casserole dish. Peel and dice the potatoes into croûton-sized cubes. Toss in 1 tbsp of the oil and season well. Set aside.

2. Fry the onion in the remaining oil until softened. Add the flour, a tablespoon at a time, and mix in until all the oil is absorbed. Allow the mixture to cook for at least 1 minute.

Add the stock or water and keep cooking until the mixture thickens. Pour the onion sauce over the sausages and add the tomatoes and beans. Season with salt, pepper and Worcestershire sauce to taste.

3. Scatter the surface of the casserole with the potato cubes and bake in the oven for 30 to 40 minutes or until the potatoes are cooked through. Best eaten with a hat on the side of your head while dreaming of wide open spaces and white chocolate!

Boys' Names of the 1950s and Now

1950	2013
1. James	Oliver (Olly)
2. Robert	Jack (Jacky)
3. John	Harry ('Arry)
4. Michael	Alfie (Alf)
5. David	Joshua (Josh)
6. William	Thomas (Tommy)
7. Richard	Charles (Charlie)
8. Thomas	William (Billy)
9. Charles	James (Jimmy)
10. Stephen	Daniel (Danny)

Vegetable oil for
frying (groundnut
or beef dripping
if being very
authentic)

200g plain flour

250ml ice-cold
water

4 firm white fish
fillets (coley or cod
is best!)

Seasoned flour for
dusting

4 to 6 large floury
potatoes, peeled
and cut into chips

FISH AND CHIPS

Tender white fish fillets encased in crispy golden batter and served with chips: what could be more tempting? We always looked forward to fish and chips as this was the day we got salt and vinegar on the tables and tomato sauce too! This provided a wonderful opportunity for the more mischievous among us to indulge in a little practical joke. Leaving the lids of the ketchup bottles unscrewed for the next unsuspecting victims to cover themselves in condiment was a much anticipated joy!

1. Heat the oil in a deep saucepan until hot. Meanwhile, mix together the flour and iced water using a whisk. Use elbow grease to knock out any lumps. Turn the fish fillets in the seasoned flour and pat off any excess.

2. Fry the chips in the hot oil until soft but not coloured at all. Drain and cool on kitchen paper.

3. Reheat the oil until very hot, dip the fish fillets in the batter and lay in the oil without causing any splashes. Fry for 4 to 5 minutes until the batter is golden. (The fish will have steamed inside the batter in this time. Drain and keep warm.)

4. Return the partly cooked chips to the very hot oil for another few minutes until crispy and golden brown. Drench with salt and vinegar while still hot and add a dollop of ketchup if you like.

TELL US A JOKE, MISS

Did you hear about the shoplifter who stole a calendar?

He got twelve months!

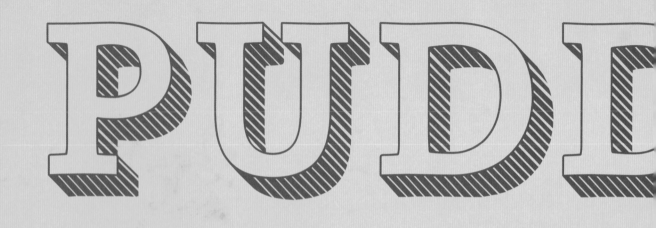

INGS

School puddings are the stuff of legends. From Great British classics such as jam roly-poly, apple pie and semolina pudding to unique school desserts like butterscotch tart and tapioca pudding, school cooks added to the excitement in the canteen every day with the variety of puds at their disposal. Custards of various colours and flavours always flowed freely and, yes, all the children (and teachers!) still titttered when they asked for 'spotted dick'.

Each recipe feeds a family of four with seconds.

MANCHESTER TART

A crisp pastry case spread with jam and filled with thick creamy custard, finished with a sprinkling of sweet coconut, Manchester tart was a school dinner favourite. It was also a fantastic way to use up any leftover pastry, jam and custard.

Seedless jam (red!)
Custard powder
Caster sugar
600ml milk
Desiccated
   coconut

Pastry
250g plain flour,
   plus extra for
   rolling out
125g butter or
   margarine

1. Preheat the oven to 200°C/Gas 6. To make the pastry, place the flour and fat in a large bowl and rub in until the mixture resembles breadcrumbs. Using a round-bladed palette knife, stir in cold water, a little at a time, until the mixture forms a dough. Use your hands to shape the pastry into a ball. Wrap in clingfilm and rest in the fridge for half an hour.

2. On a floured surface, roll out the pastry and use to line a greased tin, 36 x 20cm. Prick the pastry all over with a fork, line with greaseproof paper and fill with baking beans. Bake blind for 15 minutes.

3. Remove the baking beans and greaseproof paper and bake for a further 5 minutes. Once cool, spread the pastry case with the jam of your choice. I suggest something red and seedless!

4. Make up the custard using the custard powder, sugar and milk, according to packet instructions, and allow to cool slightly. Pour the custard over the jammy base and sprinkle with coconut. This will prevent a skin forming on the custard as well as giving it a lovely taste. Cool completely and serve with cream or more custard if you can stomach it!

Inventions to Impress Your School Chums.

How many did you know?

1. **The bicycle was invented by...**
   Kirkpatrick Macmillan (UK) in 1839.

2. **The helicopter was invented by...**
   Etienne Oehmichen (France) in 1924.

3. **The hovercraft was invented by...**
   Sir Christopher Cockerell (UK) in 1952.

4. **The jet engine was invented by...**
   Sir Frank Whittle (UK) in 1937.

5. **The laser was invented by...**
   Dr. Charles H. Townes (USA) in 1960.

To be continued...

JAM TART

With this recipe the school cooks followed the time-honoured rule of keeping it simple, but that didn't detract from my love of the jam tart. I always wanted a piece from the middle (more jam and less pastry!).

Seedless jam
(see step 2)

Pastry
250g plain flour
125g butter or
margarine

1. Preheat the oven to 200°C/Gas 6. Follow steps 1 and 2 of the instructions on page 58 for making and cooking the pastry case. Remove the baking beans and paper, bake for a further 5 minutes. Allow to cool.

2. Once cool, spread the pastry case with the jam of your choice. For ease of eating I suggest something red and seedless, but if you want to make a traffic-light tart use red, orange and green jam or marmalade arranged in blobs: the choice is yours!

PLEASE SIR, CAN I HAVE SOME MORE?

The variation on the theme was traffic-light tart, a kaleidoscope of red, orange and green blobs of jam, which I imagine allowed the cooks to use-up all the half-used pots. The lucky ones among us got a piece of tart with all three colours on it. Serve with custard and, yes, I do want the skin, please!

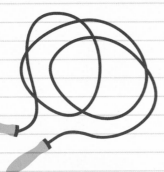

POP MUSIC

1. Can you name the four members of the band Coldplay.
2. In what year did the Beatles split up?
3. Can you name the three members of Bananarama?
4. Madonna's first hit single was...?
5. How old was Justin Bieber when he released his first single?
6. What boy band did Justin Timberlake used to sing for?
7. What was the title of Michael Jackson's movie, released after his death?
8. Who released the song 'The Cave' in 2009?
9. What are Chaz and Dave's surnames?
10. What was the first music video played on MTV?

Check the answers on pages 94–5

Jam (your choice!)
125g caster sugar
125g golden syrup
125g butter
220g cornflakes

Pastry
250g plain flour,
   plus extra for
   rolling out
125g butter or
   margarine

CORNFLAKE TART

I wish to goodness that I had learned to cook cornflake tart at school, rather than the ubiquitous fairy cakes. Golden and sparkly, this pudding was the jewel in the crown, the treasure at the end of the rainbow. Cornflake tart is a true gangster's moll of tarts: a deep, crusty and initially unyielding exterior with a surprisingly sweet layer inside. This is still a guilty pleasure today.

1. Preheat the oven to 200°C/Gas 6. Follow steps 1 and 2 of the instructions on page 58 for making and cooking the pastry case.

2. Turn the oven down to 180°C/Gas 4. Spread the pastry case with jam. Place the sugar, syrup and butter in a large pan and heat gently until the butter has melted. Give the mixture a good stir, then add the cornflakes, a handful at a time. Stir until they are all sticky.

3. Place the cornflakes on top of the jam and press down well with the back of a spoon to make an even layer. Bake in the oven for 10 minutes, then allow to cool completely before cutting into squares. For a full school dinner effect, serve with pink custard.

DID YOU KNOW?

The very first cornflake cereal, invented by the now-famous Mr Kellogg, was made available to buy in 1909!

Even More Inventions to Impress Your School Chums.

Continued from p59

1. **The microphone was invented by...**
   Alexander Graham Bell (USA) in 1876.

2. **The motorcycle was invented by...**
   Etienne Oehmichen (France) in 1924.

3. **The submarine was invented by...**
   David Bushnell (USA) in 1776.

4. **The television was invented by...**
   John Logie Baird (UK) in 1926.

5. **The thermometer was invented by...**
   Galileo Galilei (Italy) in 1593.

JAM ROLY-POLY

What a pudding jam roly-poly was: it was capable of keeping you as warm as a balaclava and mittens on strings. This is the quintessential school pudding, the one everyone recalls with fondness and a rumbling tummy. The volcanically hot spiral of jam was tempered by the soft yielding suet crust, and the whole submerged beneath lashings of lovely custard. Not requiring the slow steaming of some of the other suet puddings, this is a relatively quick, effortless and delicious recipe. It's the ideal dessert for after a chaotic Sunday roast lunch.

75g suet
150g plain flour
1 tsp baking
   powder
4 tbsp seedless
   jam (raspberry
   or strawberry)

1. Preheat the oven to 200°C/Gas 6. Using a round-bladed palette knife, mix together the dry ingredients in a mixing bowl. Add a little water at a time to bring the mixture together to form a soft dough. Use your hands to lift the mixture from the bowl and gently shape into a ball.

2. Roll or pat out the dough into a rectangle about 20 x 30cm. Spread with the jam, then dampen the edges with a little water. Roll into a log shape and place in a lightly buttered rectangular baking tin, big enough to fit the jam roly poly!

3. Bake for 30 to 40 minutes until risen and golden. Serve with lashings of custard and extra warmed jam, if so desired.

PLEASE SIR, CAN I HAVE SOME MORE?

For a syrup sponge roll, substitute the jam for the same quantity of golden syrup. Stir a couple of tablespoons of fresh white bread-crumbs into the syrup to help it stay put in the roll and not escape all over the baking tray, when heated.

INGREDIENTS

75g plain flour
80g suet
1 tsp baking powder
100g fresh
   breadcrumbs
60g soft brown sugar
150g currants or
   raisins, soaked in
   cold tea or water
About 60ml milk

SPOTTED DICK

Light as a feather and studded with sweet currants or raisins, this steamed suet pudding was the backbone of the school pudding repertoire and a great treat on a cold day. The name of this British classic could raise either a smile or a look of horror, which is why it is often known today as 'spotted dog'. This pudding taught us that if you laughed too loudly you may have to explain to everyone in the queue exactly what you found so funny. Giggle inwardly and get over it.

1. Using a round-bladed palette knife, combine together the dry ingredients in a mixing bowl. Stir in the soaked fruit. Adding a little milk at a time, bring together the mixture to form a soft dough. Use your hands to lift it from the bowl and gently shape into a log.

2. Lay out a sheet of greaseproof paper long enough to go around the pudding at least twice. Pleat several times to allow the pudding to expand. Wrap up the pudding and repeat using foil, pleating again to prevent explosions.

3. Seal well and lower into simmering water. Simmer for 90 minutes. Remove carefully and drain. Open with care as steam burns. Slice and serve with custard, cream or ice cream.

MATHS

NO CHEATING WITH A CALCULATOR!

1. $9 + 11 + 15 + 37 =$
2. $1 + 76 - 13 / 7 =$
3. $476 - 35 + 901 / 8 + 7 =$
4. $44 / 4 =$
5. $17 + 17 + 17 + 17 + 17 + 1 + 7 =$
6. $308 \times 4 - 13 =$
7. $7 \times 5 \times 5 / 3 =$
8. $1 \times 2 \times 3 \times 4 \times 5 \times 6 =$
9. $987 - 654 - 321 =$
10. $123 \times 456 \times 789 =$

GOOD LUCK!

Check the answers on pages 94–5

TELL US A JOKE, MISS

What time does Wimbledon close?

Tennish!

100ml milk
170g butter
170g soft brown
   sugar
35g plain flour

Pastry
250g plain flour,
   plus extra for
   rolling out
125g butter or
   margarine

BUTTERSCOTCH TART

Any dessert that sticks to the roof of your mouth with such soft gooeyness deserves to be as fondly remembered as this pudding. The mere thought of butterscotch tart makes my fillings ache and my tummy rumble. And the way the hot custard slightly melted the cold butterscotch filling was the stuff of dreams. Serve with hot custard or cool crème fraîche.

1. Preheat the oven to 200°C/Gas 6. Follow steps 1 and 2 of the instructions on page 58 for making and cooking the pastry case. Remove the baking beans and paper, bake for a further 5 minutes. Allow to cool.

2. Put the milk and butter in a large saucepan and place over a gentle heat. Once the butter has melted, bring the mixture to the boil. Add the sugar, stir well, then sift in the flour.

Using a wooden spoon or balloon whisk, beat well until the mixture is smooth and lump-free.

3. Simmer gently for 2 or 3 minutes; keep your arms and any small children out of the way as this can be temperamental. Beat again until the mixture becomes a little grainy and lighter in colour – a minute or two should be enough. Leave to cool.

4. When cool, spread inside the pastry case and refrigerate until cold. Serve with plenty of hot custard. Do not be tempted to cut this up while it is still warm as there will be a really sticky mess in the kitchen!

TOP 10

My Favourite Animal Families!

1. **Badger** – boar, sow, cub
2. **Sheep** – ram, ewe, lamb
3. **Cat** – tomcat, queen, kitten
4. **Deer** – stag, doe, fawn
5. **Dolphin** – bull, cow, calf
6. **Fox** – dog-fox, vixen, cub
7. **Goose** – gander, goose, gosling
8. **Pig** – boar, sow, farrow
9. **Mouse** – buck, doe, kitten
10. **Bee** – drone, queen/worker, larva

2 navel oranges
1 lemon, juiced
225g caster sugar
75g butter
3 medium eggs,
  well beaten
100g dark chocolate

Pastry
250g plain flour,
  plus extra for
  rolling out
125g butter or
  margarine

JAFFA TART

For decades now, Jaffa cakes have been a huge treat for children and so has jaffa tart, the school pudding equivalent. The orangey base was tangy and gooey and topped with grated chocolate, which melted into a wonderful brown slick when the tart was served with hot custard. The orange layer is a basic orange curd, which is simple to make. You will have some left over to make a second tart or to enjoy on your morning toast. If only school cooks had thought of a way to make a pudding version of iced gems and chocolate fingers my world would have been complete.

1. Preheat the oven to 200°C/Gas 6. Follow steps 1 and 2 of the instructions on page 58 for making and cooking the pastry case. Remove the baking beans and paper, bake for a further 5 minutes. Allow to cool.

2. To make the orange curd, grate the rind from one of the oranges and place in a heatproof bowl. Add the juice from both oranges and the lemon juice. Add the sugar, butter and eggs and place the bowl over a pan of barely simmering water. Heat gently, whisking all the time, until the curd mixture thickens. Leave to cool.

3. Once cool, spread the pastry case with the orange curd. Any remaining curd can be kept refrigerated for up to a week.

4. Grate the chocolate over the tart and keep refrigerated until needed. Serve with warm custard or very cold cream.

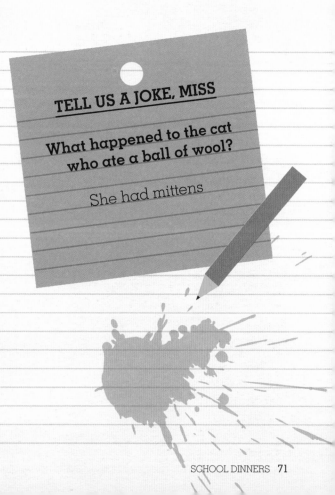

TELL US A JOKE, MISS

What happened to the cat who ate a ball of wool?

She had mittens

10g (one pack) of
strawberry jelly
410g (a small can)
evaporated
milk (refrigerated)
125g caster sugar
125g golden syrup
125g butter
220g cornflakes

Pastry
250g plain flour,
plus extra for
rolling out
125g butter or
margarine

PINK SLICE AND CORNFLAKES

A magnificent, if unusual, concoction served only in schools, pink slice and cornflakes was eagerly anticipated by everyone. Especially me. Eat it and weep! And then have seconds...

1. Preheat the oven to 200°C/Gas 6. Follow steps 1 and 2 of the instructions on page 58 for making and cooking the pastry case. Remove the baking beans and paper, bake for a further 5 minutes. Allow to cool.

2. Dissolve the jelly in 150ml boiling water and then add 150ml cool water. This is now double strength! Do not panic. Place in the fridge until just setting around the edges.

3. Remove the jelly and the evaporated milk from the fridge. Place the milk in a bowl and whisk until frothy. Add the barely set jelly and whisk again until very bubbly. Pour the pink mousse on to the pastry base and leave in the fridge until set.

4. Place the sugar, syrup and butter in a large pan and heat gently until the butter has melted. Stir and add the cornflakes a few at a time. Mix well and place on top of the mousse. Serve immediately.

TOP 10

Excuses For Being Late to Class

1. The school bell rings before I get there!
2. I saw a sign that read 'School Ahead. Go Slow'.
3. My watch was set to a different time zone.
4. I had to feed my pet elephant.
5. My alarm clock kept going off while I was asleep.
6. Sorry – usually my punctuation skills are excellent.
7. I was dreaming about a football game, and it went into extra time.
8. I was on time – everyone else was early!
9. I told you if I wasn't here, you should go ahead and start without me.
10. I thought I could stay late and make up the hours.

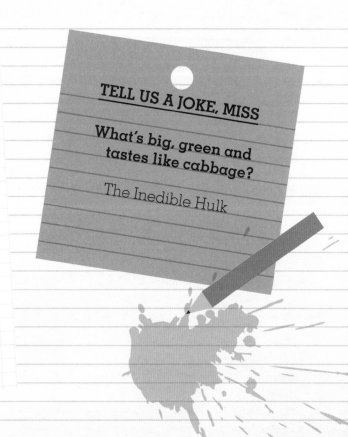

TELL US A JOKE, MISS

What's big, green and tastes like cabbage?

The Inedible Hulk

4 large Bramley
    apples
Splash of water
Knob of butter
Golden caster sugar
1 tsp ground
    cinnamon or a
    few cloves
A handful of raisins
Caster sugar for
    sprinkling

<u>Pastry</u>
250g plain flour
125g butter or
    margarine

APPLE PIE

Apple pie's simplicity is what makes it taste so good. As does the vast quantity of custard you will need to make, as I can guarantee everyone will want seconds. Such a classic dish requires love and attention if you want to achieve perfection, so take the time to get the flavours just right. This is the perfect winter weekend treat and will encourage the children to eat lots of lovely healthy fruit. It is also wonderful served with a few spoonfuls of vanilla ice cream.

1. Preheat the oven to 200°C/Gas 6. Follow step 1 of the instructions on page 58 for making the pastry.

2. Peel and core the apples. Cut into generous chunks and place in a saucepan with a splash of water, a knob of butter and sugar to taste. Gently cook the apples until the edges of each piece just begin to soften. Put the part-cooked apples into a large baking dish and top with a little more sugar if it tastes very sharp. Sprinkle with cinnamon or a few cloves and the raisins.

3. Roll out the pastry and cover the apple mixture. Sprinkle the surface of the pie with caster sugar and make a small slit in the pie crust to let steam escape. Bake for 20 to 30 minutes or until the pastry is golden brown and the apple inside is bubbling. Serve with custard, or ice cream if you have to.

DID YOU KNOW?

Archaeologists discovered evidence that human beings have been enjoying apples since at least 6500BC.

A selection of fruit
to fill the bottom of
a large baking dish
(choose from
rhubarb, plum,
apricot, apple
or pear)
Caster sugar to
taste

Topping
250g plain flour
125g butter or
margarine
125g sugar

FRUIT CRUMBLE

If the school cook had a plum tree in her garden we were sure to
get plum crumble at least once a fortnight until the glut was over,
and we were very happy about it. Crumbles were as seasonal as
puddings could come. Chewy and crunchy at the same time, this
is heaven on an aluminium spoon. The recipe works well with a
wide range of different fruits, including plums, apples, pears,
apricots and rhubarb. Use whatever is in season.

1. Preheat the oven to 200°C/Gas 6. Cut up the fruit into manageable pieces and lay in the bottom of a large and deep baking dish. Be generous. Try a small piece of fruit and add sugar to taste. You can liven up this dish with spices if you like. Rhubarb works well with ginger, apples go well with cinnamon and pears love a splash of red wine.

2. Place the flour, fat and sugar into a separate bowl and rub together with your finger tips until the mix resembles breadcrumbs. Sprinkle this mixture over the fruit and bake for 30 minutes until the fruit is bubbling away and the topping is golden. Leave to stand for a few minutes before serving. The word volcanic is not an exaggeration! Serve with custard.

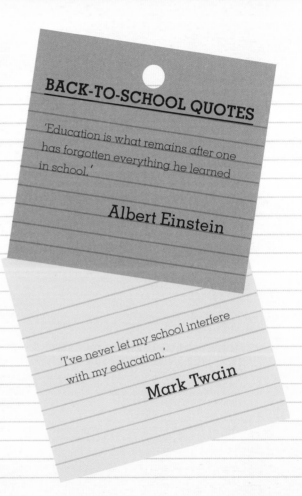

BACK-TO-SCHOOL QUOTES

'Education is what remains after one has forgotten everything he learned in school.'

Albert Einstein

'I've never let my school interfere with my education.'

Mark Twain

600ml full-fat milk
25g caster sugar
40g semolina
25g butter
Grated nutmeg

SEMOLINA PUDDING

This baked milk pudding was another traditional favourite. Creamy and smooth, it was served with jam or fruit compôte. We could never decide whether to stir the jam into the semolina, eat the blob of jam first, or save it for the last sweet fruity mouthful. However we ate it, this pudding was always warm and familiar, the perfect comfort food to help us through the challenges of a hectic afternoon.

1. Preheat the oven to 150°C/Gas 2. Heat the milk and sugar in a pan until warmed. Gently tip in the semolina a little at a time, stirring continuously. We are not trying to re-create this dish with the lumps!

2. Add the butter, stir until melted and allow to simmer for 10 minutes until thickened. Place in a large buttered dish, sprinkle the top with nutmeg and bake in the oven for 30 to 40 minutes. Serve with jam or fruit compôte. Alternatively, serve straight from the dish into bowls and add grated chocolate as a decoration.

PHILOSOPHY
WHO SAID WHAT?

1. 'I think therefore I am'
2. 'I don't know why we are here, but I'm pretty sure it is not in order to enjoy ourselves'
3. 'We live in the best of all possible worlds'
4. 'God is dead'
5. 'One cannot step twice in the same river'
6. 'He who thinks great thoughts, often makes great errors'
7. 'Happiness is not an ideal of reason but of imagination'
8. 'Leisure is the mother of philosophy'
9. 'Science is what you know. Philosophy is what you don't know'
10. 'The only thing I know is that I know nothing'

Check the answers on pages 94–5!

DID YOU KNOW?

The word semolina is derived from the Italian word for flour, semola.

150g plain flour
50g cocoa powder
100g golden syrup
100g soft brown
  sugar
100g butter
1 tsp milk
1 tsp bicarbonate
  of soda
1 medium egg,
  beaten

CHOCOLATE SPONGE

So many people cite school chocolate sponge as the beginning of their love of all things chocolate. Try this recipe and you will see why. Served hot with mint custard, this heavenly pudding is just light enough to leave room for seconds.

1. Preheat the oven to 190°C/Gas 5 and line a rectangular tin, 20 x 30cm, with greaseproof paper. In a large mixing bowl, sift the flour and cocoa powder together.

2. Place the golden syrup, brown sugar and butter in a saucepan and stir all of the mixture over a gentle heat until the butter has melted. Remove from the heat, allow to cool slightly, then add the milk. Stir in the bicarbonate of soda and egg, mix well.

3. Stir the wet ingredients into the sifted flour and cocoa, beating well to ensure the mixture is smooth. Pour into the tin and bake for 20 to 25 minutes. Turn the cake out onto a wire rack to cool slightly. Once cooled, cut into generous squares and serve with mint custard.

TELL US A JOKE, MISS

What did the grocer say when he ran out of onions?

That's shallot!

QUIZ TIME

LANGUAGES

Can you translate these simple phrases into English?

1. 'Ou est la poubelle?' (French)
2. 'Hvordan har du det I dag?' (Danish)
3. 'Ho perso la mia borsa' (Italian)
4. '¿De dónde eres' (Spanish)
5. 'Jaké je vaše jméno?' (Czech)
6. 'Možete li mi pomoci molim vas?' (Croatian)
7. 'Ik ben verloren!' (Dutch)
8. 'A keni kohë?' (Albanian)
9. 'Talarðu ensku?' (Icelandic)
10. 'Hvor kan jeg kjøpe litt mat?' (Norwegian)

Check the answers on pages 94–5!

PINEAPPLE UPSIDE-DOWN CAKE

For us pineapple upside-down cake was exotic and exciting. Rings of succulent pineapple and glacé cherries topped the moist sponge, but the best bit was the much-loved sticky coating over the top of the cake. Glacé cherry lovers chose their seats carefully. Nestling between several cherry haters could gain you up to half a dozen extra red jewels on your plate. Taking the time to eat around the pineapple ring, saving the juice-drenched sponge underneath until last, was utter bliss.

2 tbsp soft brown sugar
1 can pineapple rings
Glacé cherries
3 eggs, weighed in their shells
An equivalent weight of butter
An equivalent weight of caster sugar
An equivalent weight of self-raising flour
1 tbsp pineapple juice
½ tsp vanilla extract

1. Preheat the oven to 190°C/Gas 5 and line a 15 x 25cm rectangular tin with greaseproof paper. Sprinkle the brown sugar on to the paper and arrange the pineapple rings evenly on top. Adorn the centre of each ring with half a glacé cherry, cut side up for the best aesthetics.

2. In a large bowl, cream together the butter and sugar until the mixture becomes paler in colour and lighter in texture. Beat the eggs in one at a time. If the mixture starts to look a little grainy add a spoonful of the flour. Fold in the remaining flour carefully, then stir in the pineapple juice and vanilla extract.

3. Spoon the mixture into the tin evenly and smooth out, trying not to disturb the cherries. Bake for 30 to 35 minutes or until golden and well risen. Leave to cool for 5 minutes. Turn out of the tin and carefully peel back the paper to reveal the cake in all its golden and glistening glory.

TELL US A JOKE, MISS

What did the biscuit scream when it was run over?

Crumbs!

50g pudding rice
  or tapioca
25g butter
600ml full-fat milk
25g caster sugar
Nutmeg

RICE OR TAPIOCA PUDDING

I confess to being a lover of milk puddings. The creaminess and the warmth are so lovely. While I preferred the texture of rice to tapioca, I was more than happy to eat either of them. What really made it for me was the swirl of rosehip syrup or blob of jam. Never a stirrer, I always ate around the sweet jammy dollop and slowly savoured it long after my friends had left to do handstands up against the playground wall.

1. Preheat the oven to 150°C/Gas 2. If you are using rice, rinse it in water and drain. Place the rice or tapioca in a large buttered ovenproof dish and stir in the milk and sugar. Dot with the remaining butter and place in the oven for 1 hour, stirring every 15 minutes.

2. Grate a little fresh nutmeg over the surface of the pudding and return to the oven for another hour until the surface is golden. Serve with rosehip syrup or a dollop of jam.

TOP 10

Popular Movies
Set in School

How many have you seen?

1. *Dead Poets Society*
2. *Napoleon Dynamite*
3. *The Breakfast Club*
4. *Clueless*
5. *American Pie*
6. *American Graffiti*
7. *Harry Potter I–VII*
8. *Donnie Darko*
9. *Superbad*
10. *Ferris Bueller's Day Off*

DID YOU KNOW?

Such is the importance of rice in Japanese culture, the word Gohan, to describe 'cooked rice', also means 'meal'.

250g plain flour,
plus extra for
dusting
2 tsp baking powder
1 tsp salt
110g caster sugar
Knob of butter
1 medium egg,
beaten
125ml milk
Jam for filling
Vegetable oil for
frying
Caster sugar for
dusting

DOUGHNUTS

So many happy lunch hours were passed trying to eat a doughnut without licking our lips. We all knew this was an impossible task but were thankful for the opportunity to have a go. Filled with oozing jam, or ring-shaped and dusted with crunchy sugar, doughnuts were a welcome treat. They were often served at school with milky coffee, which seems a little surprising these days. Serve warm for the ultimate indulgence.

1. Mix together the dry ingredients in a bowl. Add the butter and rub in until the mixture resembles fine breadcrumbs. Stir in the egg and enough milk to make a soft but not too sticky dough. Dust a board with flour and tip the dough on to this. Flour the top of the dough and either push or roll out until the dough is 2.5cm thick.

2. For jam doughnuts, use a large round cutter to cut out rounds. Place a spoonful of jam in the middle and pinch the top of the doughnut closed into a ball shape. Roll in your hands to really close the dough.

3. Heat a frying pan containing 2.5cm of vegetable oil. Fry the doughnuts gently on all sides until golden brown. Drain on kitchen paper and toss in a little more sugar to coat. Sit with friends and family and try to eat a whole doughnut without licking your lips.

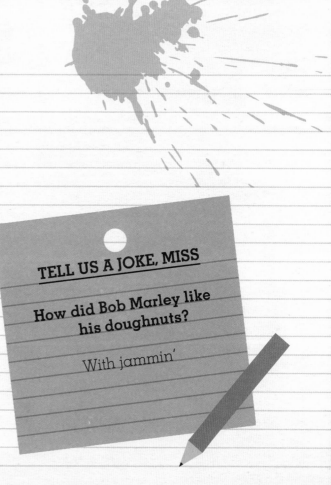

TELL US A JOKE, MISS

How did Bob Marley like his doughnuts?

With jammin'

150ml warm water

60g caster sugar

1 sachet yeast

650g strong white
  bread flour, plus
  extra for rolling out

1 tsp salt

75g white vegetable
  fat

180ml warm milk

1 medium egg,
  beaten

150g icing sugar

Food colouring

Cocoa powder

ICED FINGERS

These delicious sticky buns came with a few variations: white icing, pink icing or rarely, but always longed for, chocolate icing. I even have a vague memory of there being red, white and blue buns at school for the Queen's Silver Jubilee in 1977. This was another dilemma dish for me: should I lick off the icing first, eat the bun first and have the icing last, or just stuff the whole lot in and be done with it? Usually I went for the latter as it was too tempting to have the bun looking at me as I tried to make a decision.

1. Place the warm water in a jug and stir in a sprinkling of sugar and the yeast. Leave in a warm place until the yeast has doubled in size.

2. Sift the flour into a mixing bowl and stir in the remaining sugar and salt. Cut the vegetable fat into the flour and rub in until the mixture resembles breadcrumbs. Pour in the warm milk and stir to begin to incorporate, then add the beaten egg and the yeast mixture. Using a round-bladed palette knife, mix until the dough comes together.

3. Using your hands, knead the dough gently but effectively on a floured surface for 5 minutes or so until it becomes smooth and silky. The dough is very soft and 'loose' so you may need more flour on your work surface as you work it. Shape into a ball and place in an oiled bowl. Cover with a damp cloth and leave for an hour and a half until well risen. Knock back the dough, then let it rise again for another 45 minutes.

4. On a lightly floured surface, divide the mixture into cricket-ball sized pieces. Roll out into sausage shapes and place on an oiled baking sheet to rise again for another 15 minutes. Meanwhile, preheat the oven to 190°C/Gas 5.

5. Bake for 15 minutes and leave to cool. When cool, mix the icing sugar with a little water and some food colouring or cocoa to make a runny icing. Apply to the tops of the buns with a 2.5cm paintbrush, or use a teaspoon. If you do use a brush, buy a new one!

200g golden syrup
25g butter
50g breadcrumbs
Grated rind and
   juice of ½ lemon

Pastry
250g plain flour
125g butter or
   margarine

TREACLE TART

Finely balanced between cloying sweetness and sharp sourness, the treacle tart is a wonder among puddings and ridiculously easy to make. It is delightfully chewy and such a good way to soak up the custard served with it. The hint of lemon probably went straight over our heads as youngsters but it is what makes treacle tart the pudding it is now.

1. Preheat the oven to 200°C/Gas 6. Follow step 1 of the instructions on page 58 for making the pastry. Line a small 15 x 15cm cake tin with pastry (you can use a small pie dish if you wish.) Treacle tarts often came with a lattice top, so if you feel like gilding the lily, re-roll the pastry trimmings and cut into 2.5cm wide strips.

2. Warm the syrup and butter together gently in a pan. Add the breadcrumbs, lemon rind and juice – stir to combine. Pour the syrup sludge into the pastry case and use the strips to form a lattice. I have had them with twisted lattices, very complex woven lattices, and I believe you can even buy a special roller to cut the pastry lattice for you. Please do as you see fit.

3. Trim the pie edges and bake for 30 minutes. Serve warm with thick custard.

TOP 10

Reasons why school is amazing!

1. The potential excitement of snowy days.
2. Making new friends every year.
3. Covering school books in wrapping paper.
4. Playing football after school until the sun goes down.
5. Seeing that boy/girl you have a crush on.
6. The tuck shop at lunchtime.
7. School discos at the end of term.
8. Changing out of your school uniform.
9. Summer holidays.
10. School dinners!

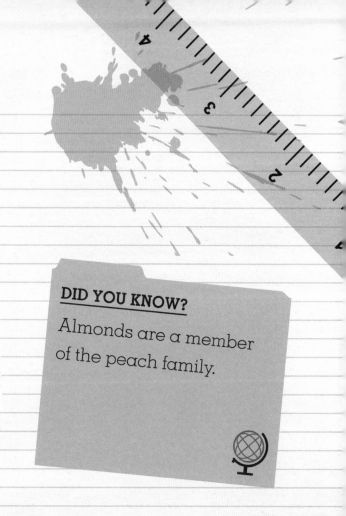

DID YOU KNOW?

Almonds are a member of the peach family.

125g caster sugar

125g golden syrup

25g cocoa powder, sifted

125g butter

220g cornflakes

Smarties

CHOCOLATE CORNFLAKE CAKES

Each adorned with a single Smartie, these crunchy cakes were a real end-of-term treat.

1. Line a patty tin with paper cake cases. Place the sugar, syrup, cocoa and butter in a large pan and heat gently until the butter has melted. Give the mixture a good stir and add the cornflakes a few handfuls at a time. Mix well to make sure each cornflake is sticky.

2. Spoon the cornflake mix into the cake cases. Fill each case generously and press down a little to ensure the cornflakes stick together. Decorate each cornflake cake with a Smartie. Refrigerate until the cakes have cooled and become hard.

3. Fight with your best friend for the last cake with an orange Smartie.

PINK CUSTARD

Lurid in colour, luscious in texture and loved almost universally, pink custard made a simple iced sponge into a proper pudding.

1 packet pink blancmange mix
2 or 3 tbsp caster sugar to taste
600ml milk, plus a little extra if needed

1. Empty the blancmange mix into a heatproof bowl. Add the sugar and 2 or 3 tablespoons of the milk and mix to a paste.

2. Heat the remaining milk in a pan until warm but not boiling. Pour a little of the milk on to the paste and give it a really good mix. Stir this bright pink goo into the warmed milk and then bring to the boil. Keep stirring and simmer for about a minute. If the custard is very thick, add a little more milk to thin it.

3. Serve with iced vanilla or chocolate sponge. Any leftovers (a rare event!) can be kept in the fridge and served cold the next day.

ANSWERS!

Science p. 21
1. Carbon
2. The femur (or thighbone)
3. Liquid Crystal Display
4. A Fibonacci Series
5. Protons and Neutrons
6. Lactose
7. The jaguar
8. X-rays
9. Cosine
10. Blue

Geography p. 33
1. The Balearic Islands
2. Peru
3. Washington DC
4. The Zambezi
5. The Dead Sea
6. An oxbow lake
7. Singapore
8. Lebanon
9. The Indian Ocean
10. Gerard Mercator

Entertainment p. 41
1. 'Mad Men'
2. 'Goodfellas'
3. Bon Jovi
4. Montague and Capulet
5. Lt Theo Kojak
6. Russell Crowe ('Gladiator')
7. Aaron
8. Casablanca
9. Gustav Holst
10. Kasabian

Art and Literature p. 51
1. Jackson Pollock
2. 'Pride and Prejudice'
3. Auguste Rodin
4. King Lear
5. 'Little Women'
6. Frans Hals
7. The pilgrims in Chaucer's 'The Canterbury Tales'
8. Aphrodite
9. Porcelain
10. Stephenie Meyer

Pop Music p.61
1. Chris Martin, Jonny Buckland, Guy Berryman and Will Champion
2. 1970
3. Sarah Dallin, Siobhan Fahey and Keren Woodward.
4. 'Holiday'
5. 16
6. N*S*Y*N*C
7. This Is It
8. Mumford & Sons
9. Hodges & Peacock
10. 'Video Killed the Radio Star' by The Buggles

Maths p.67
1. 72
2. 9.14
3. 174.75
4. 11
5. 93
6. 1, 219
7. 58.3333333333